Treats

Written by Jay Kenerly • Illustrated by Tracey J. Marshall • Edited by Rosemary Plybon

No part of this publication may be reproduced
or transmitted in any form or by any means,
electronic or mechanical, including photocopy, recording,
or any information storage and
retrieval system, without permission in writing from the author,
illustrator, and/or publisher.

Copyright © 2013 Jay Kenerly
All rights reserved.
ISBN-13: 978-0615841908

DEDICATED TO:

Rose, Hal, Bert, Maye and Viv...they give me many more "treats" than I could ever give them.

Red...he turned a "dog guy" into a "cat guy" over night.

Lily...she reminds me every day that it is okay to be both a cat and dog guy.

IN HONOR AND MEMORY OF:

Chablis...Rest easy, sweet kitty. Heaven is full of treats.

For many reasons we love Mom the most.

Of that we are not afraid to boast.

"Why," you ask?
The list is long.
We could fill your ears
from dusk 'til dawn.

But one stands out above the rest. One reason why we know Mom is best. For when we need her most, not least, Mom is there...

We love
her most
when
there are
lots to eat.

Our favorites are the ones that taste like meats.

We don't like the taste of broccoli or beets.

But really, there are no kinds we like the least. The ones Mom gives us are our favorite treats.

So after it rains, or snows, or sleets...

Or after prowling around some scary streets...

Or after chasing mice, with their little feets...

Or fighting with dogs, those filthy beasts...

At the end of the day, when it is time to rest, we beg for one more, and Mom cannot resist.

Then she is off to bed and to sleep, and we know for sure Mom is our real treat!

Night Night

So we
snuggle next to her,
all cozy in the sheets...

And we drift off to sleep...

Made in the USA
Middletown, DE
08 May 2015